REVENUE EFFECTS OF
MAJOR TAX BILLS

by

Jerry Tempalski
U.S. Department of the Treasury

OTA Working Paper 81   **Revised September 2006**

The OTA Papers series is an occasional series of reports on the research, models, and datasets developed to inform and improve Treasury's tax policy analysis. The papers are works in progress and subject to revision. Views and opinions expressed are those of the authors and do not necessarily represent official Treasury positions or policy. OTA Papers are distributed in order to document OTA analytic methods and data and invite discussion and suggestions for revision and improvement. Comments are welcome and should be directed to the authors.

Office of Tax Analysis
U.S. Treasury Department
Washington, D.C. 20220

I am grateful to Robert Carroll, Lowell Dworin, Laura Kalambokidis, David Richardson, and Karl Scholz for their comments and to Kevin Morris and Anona Samuel for their research assistance. The views expressed in this paper are those of the author and do not necessarily represent the views of the U.S. Treasury Department.

ABSTRACT

Since 1940 many major tax bills have been enacted. This paper uses revenue estimates of each bill to create consistent measures of the relative size of the several dozen major tax bill enacted since 1940.

The Revenue Act of 1942 was the biggest tax increase (and biggest tax bill) of the 1940-1967 period; the Revenue Act of 1945 was the biggest tax cut of that period. The Economic Recovery Tax Act of 1981 was the biggest tax cut (and biggest tax bill) of the 1968-2006 period; the Tax Equity and Fiscal Responsibility Act of 1982 was the biggest tax increase of that period.

Jerry Tempalski
Office of Tax Analysis
Room 4108, Main Treasury Building
1500 Pennsylvania Avenue, N.W.
Washington, D.C. 20220
JERRY.TEMPALSKI@DO.TREAS.GOV

REVENUE EFFECTS OF MAJOR TAX BILLS

Since the federal income tax was significantly expanded in 1940, several dozen major tax bills have been enacted. Inevitably, discussions (and disagreements) have arisen concerning the relative size of the bills' effects on federal revenues.[1] This paper uses revenue estimates from Treasury and the Joint Committee on Taxation to compare the relative size of the revenue effect of the major tax bills enacted after 1939 using four different measures. An appendix provides a short list of the major provisions in the bills.

The paper divides the post-1939 years into two periods, 1940-1967 and 1968-2006. The comparison of tax bills for the first period should be examined with some caution, because the revenue estimates are from different sources and are not completely consistent. The comparison for the second period can be viewed with more confidence, because the estimates are relatively consistent.

Comparing the size of the revenue effects of tax bills sounds like a relatively easy exercise. But because the available data are not necessarily consistent and because there are several ways of measuring the revenue effects of tax bills, problems have to be resolved and choices have to be made before the bills can be compared. Each section discusses some of the problems encountered and choices made in comparing the revenue estimates.

This paper analyzes each tax bill separately. A bill is analyzed on the basis of exactly those provisions contained in the bill when the bill was enacted. Bills are not analyzed together, even if a later bill was primarily designed to offset some of the effect of an earlier bill. For example, although the Tax Equity and Fiscal Responsibility Act of 1982 (TEFRA) was enacted

---

[1] See for example, Louis Lyons, "TEFRA '82 vs. OBRA '93: Whose Tax Increase Was Bigger?" Tax Notes, August 26, 1996, pp. 1098-1099.

primarily to offset some of the revenue loss from the Economic Recovery Tax Act of 1981 (ERTA), the two bills are analyzed as separate bills in this paper.

The four measures used to compare the revenue estimates of the tax bills are:

- current dollars,

- constant 1992 dollars,

- percentage of gross domestic product (GDP),

- percentage of total federal receipts.

The single best measure for most purposes is probably the revenue effect as a percentage of GDP, because it eliminates the effects of inflation, real economic growth, and the size of total federal receipts. The second best measure is probably constant dollars, because it eliminates the effects of inflation and the size of total federal receipts.

1940-1967

Congressional floor discussions indicate that most of the major tax bills in the 1940-1967 period were associated with wars.[2] The tax increases in the 1940-1943 period helped pay for the costs of preparing for, and fighting, World War II. The Revenue Act of 1945 cut taxes in the aftermath of World War II. The tax increases in 1950 and 1951 were passed to pay for the Korean War, and the Tax Adjustment Act of 1966 helped to pay for the Vietnam War.

---

[2] The Congressional Record contains all Congressional floor discussions.

Methodology - For each tax bill of this period, Treasury and the Joint Committee on Taxation (JCT)[3] presumably produced revenue estimates.[4] A consistent source of revenue estimates, however, was not available for all bills from this period. For some bills, Treasury Department estimates were available. For other bills, JCT estimates were available. For still other bills, the only estimates available were from statements or tables included in the Congressional Record without a citation for the source of the estimates. For this subsection, Treasury estimates were used when available. Table 1 notes which estimates are not Treasury estimates.

For some bills, revenue estimates for the year after enactment were available. For others, "full-year effect" estimates were available. Full-year effect estimates were used when available. Table 1 notes which estimates are for the year after enactment.

Actual GDP and GDP deflator figures for the year after enactment were used to estimate a bill's constant dollar effect and its effect as a percentage of GDP. Similarly, actual federal revenues for the year after enactment were used to estimate a bill's effect as a percentage of federal revenue.

---

[3] Before 1974 the JCT was known as the Joint Committee on Internal Revenue Taxation.

[4] The two group's estimates historically are generally close to each other.

Results - By all measures, the Revenue Act of 1942 was by far the biggest tax increase of the period and was also bigger than any tax decrease of the period, making it the biggest tax bill of the period. (See Table 1 and Figures 1 and 2.) The second biggest tax increase of the period, measured as a percentage of GDP, was the Revenue Act of 1941. Measured in constant dollars, however, the Revenue Act of 1951 was the second largest tax increase.

Measured as a percentage of GDP, the Revenue Act of 1945 was the biggest tax cut of the period, with the Revenue Act of 1948 the second biggest tax cut. Measured in constant dollars, however, the Revenue Act of 1964 was the biggest tax cut, with the Revenue Act of 1945 second.

1968-2006

The revenue estimates for the bills in the 1968-2006 period suggest that the period can broken into three subperiods. First, most of the bills enacted before 1982 were tax cuts. During this period, inflation was relatively high and the individual income tax parameters were not indexed for inflation. Without indexation, inflation can push taxpayers into higher tax brackets without any increase in real income. This phenomenon is called "bracket creep," and it increases federal revenue as a percentage of GDP without any legislative action. In fact, when inflation is relatively high and bracket creep is particularly intense, as it was through much of the 1970's, policymakers have to cut taxes repeatedly to maintain the desired level of taxes. Of the 9 major tax bills enacted between 1968 and 1981, 6 reduced federal revenue.

Second, in 1981, ERTA was enacted, which provided for the indexation of the individual income tax parameters. The combination of indexation and relatively large federal budget deficits helped cause 9 of the 11 major tax bills enacted between 1982 and 1993 to increase federal revenue.

Third, all 8 of the major tax bills enacted after 1993 have reduced federal revenue, some as a result of soaring federal revenue in the late 1990's and early 2000's that pushed the federal budget into surplus for the first time in many years.

Methodology - For the bills in this period, Treasury Department revenue estimates were used, because inflation and GDP forecasts consistent with the Treasury estimates were more readily available than forecasts consistent with the JCT estimates. The estimates are for the federal government's fiscal years (July 1-June 30 for 1968-1976, and October 1-September 30 for post-1976 years).

Treasury revenue estimates presented in the Administration's first post-enactment January budget were used.[5][6] Treasury produces estimates for a bill when it is enacted, generally reestimates the bill for the January budget, and sometimes reestimates a bill for several subsequent budgets. In a few cases, the first post-enactment estimates proved not very accurate. For example, revenues from the Crude Oil Windfall Profit Tax of 1980 were estimated to be $21

---

[5] The first post-enactment January budget for the Consolidated Budget and Reconciliation Act of 1985 (COBRA) did not contain the revenue effect of COBRA. COBRA estimates used in this paper are from the second post-enactment January budget.

[6] Revenue estimates for bills enacted after 1995 were not shown in the January budgets. Except for the Tax Increase Prevention and Reconciliation Act of 2005 (TIPRA), which was enacted in May 2006, internal Treasury Department estimates made in conjunction with the first post-enactment budgets are used in this paper. For TIPRA, internal Treasury estimates made in conjunction with the first post-enactment midsession review are used.

billion in 1984; actual revenues were probably less than $4 billion. This paper makes no adjustment for estimates that proved to be inaccurate.

When available, estimates are presented for each of the first 4 fiscal years after enactment. For most years, 4 years of post-enactment estimates were available; for the earliest years of the period, only 2 years of estimates were available. Annual averages for the first 4 years after enactment and the first 2 years after enactment are also presented.

Constant dollar estimates are first computed based on the calendar year GDP deflator forecast contained in the same January budget from which the revenue estimates came. Then these estimates are converted into 1992 dollars based on the actual GDP deflator. Revenue effects as a percentage of GDP are based on calendar year GDP forecasts from the same January budget.[7] Revenue effects as a percentage of total revenues are based on fiscal year federal revenue forecasts from the same January budget. The federal receipts forecasts reported in the budget are reduced by the effect of the enacted bill under analysis and by the effect of Administration's proposed legislative changes contained in the budget.

Analyzing tax bills strictly by their revenue estimates can be deceiving for at least three reasons. First, some tax bills have major provisions that are temporary (e.g., 10-percent income tax surcharge in the Revenue and Expenditure Control Act of 1968), masking the long-run effect of the tax bill for the first year or two after enactment. Other tax bills have major provisions that do not become effective until several years after enactment (e.g., the indexation of individual tax

---

[7] The first post-enactment January budgets for the Revenue and Expenditure Control Act of 1968 (RECA) and the Tax Reform Act of 1969 did not contain GDP deflator estimates nor GDP estimates for

parameters in ERTA was not effective until 1985), which also prevent the long-term effects of the tax bill from being seen in the years right after enactment. The estimates presented in this period include no adjustment to capture the long-run, fully-phased-in effect of the tax bills. With the sharp increase in the use of sunsets and phase-ins in recent legislation (e.g., Economic Growth and Tax Relief Reconciliation Act of 2001 (EGTRRA)), it is particularly difficult to compare the true long-term revenue effects of recent tax bills.

Second, relatively small differences in the effective dates of tax provisions can affect the revenue estimate for the year after enactment. For bills whose important provisions are effective before October 1 (the start of the fiscal year) of the year of enactment, the revenue estimate for the year after enactment will reflect a full year's economic activity. For bills whose important provisions are effective after October 1 -- January 1 is the effective date for many provisions -- the first year's revenue estimate will not reflect a full year's economic activity. For example, the individual tax rate cut in ERTA was not effective until January 1, 1982. Thus, the revenue estimate for fiscal year 1982 only contains a 9-month effect. On the other hand, the individual tax rate increase in Omnibus Reconciliation Bill of 1993 (OBRA93) was retroactive, so the revenue estimate for fiscal year 1994 contains a 12-month effect.

---

the second year after enactment. As a substitute for these missing estimates, the actual figures were used.

Third, government revenue estimates do not take into account the effect of the bills on GDP, even though some bills (e.g., Tax Reduction Act of 1975) were primarily designed to stimulate the economy.[8] The effect of most tax bills on GDP is uncertain, but probably generally small.[9]

Results - By every measure used here, ERTA was by far the biggest tax change (and the biggest tax cut) over the past 35 years. (See Table 2 and Figures 3 and 4.) The revenue effect of ERTA was more than twice as large (in constant dollars) as any other post-1967 tax bill. Similarly, the revenue effect of ERTA, measured as a percentage of GDP and as a percentage of total federal revenue, was more than twice as large as any post-1967 tax bill, except RECA, which contained a temporary 10-percent income tax surcharge. The second largest tax cut of the period as a percentage of GDP was the Revenue Act of 1978; the second largest tax cut in constant dollars was the EGTRRA.

TEFRA was the biggest tax increase of the period measured in constant dollars and as a percentage of GDP. OBRA93 was the second biggest tax increase measured in constant dollars and as a percentage of GDP.

---

[8] Indirectly, the revenue estimates in the budget may contain a small GDP effect. If an enacted bill affects the budget GDP forecast, the revenue estimate for the bill will contain a small GDP effect. The rest of the tax effect from the GDP effect will show up only as a change in baseline tax receipts.

[9] For a discussion on including the effect of tax bills on GDP in government revenue estimates, see Alan J. Auerbach, "Dynamic Revenue Estimates," The Journal of Economic Perspectives, Winter 1996, Volume 10, Number 1, pp. 141-157.

APPENDIX

This appendix provides a short list of the major provisions in each of the tax bills examined in this paper. For each bill, the provisions are listed in rough order of their revenue effects, with the provision with the greatest revenue effect listed first.

For tax bills of the World War II era (1940-1945), the descriptions of the major provisions are less detailed than the descriptions for other tax bills. The reason for this difference is that the enormous increase in the need for revenue in that era led to many different types of taxes on individual and corporate incomes. The interrelationships between these different taxes make it very difficult to briefly summarize the effects of enacted provisions.[10]

Revenue Act of 1940
- temporarily and permanently increased individual income tax rates
- temporarily and permanently increased corporate income tax rates (top rate from 19% to 22.1%)
- temporarily increased most excise tax rates to 30-50%
- reduced personal exemption amount from $2,500 to $2,000 (married couples)

Second Revenue Act of 1940
- created corporate excess profits tax (top rate of 50%)
- increased corporate income tax rates (top rate increased from 22.1% to 24%)

Revenue Act of 1941
- increased excess profits tax by 10 percentage points (top rate increased from 50% to 60%)
- permanently extended 1940 temporary individual, corporate, and excise tax increases
- increased corporate tax rates 6-7 percentage points (top rate increased from 24% to 31%)
- increased excise taxes on alcohol, tires, etc.
- reduced personal exemption amount from $2,000 to $1,500 (married couples)

Revenue Act of 1942
- increased individual income tax rates
- increased corporate tax rates (top rate increased from 31% to 40%)
- replaced 35-60% graduated rate schedule for excess profits tax with flat 90% rate
- created 5% Victory tax on all individual income over $624, with postwar credit
- reduced personal exemption amount from $1,500 to $1,200 (married couples)

---

[10] Even before 1940, the "normal" individual and corporate tax rates were supplemented with surtax rates that far exceeded the normal rates. Both the normal and the surtax rates were changed several times during the 1940-1945 period. In 1940, temporary "defeat" tax increases on individual and corporate incomes were enacted. Also in 1940, an corporate excess profits tax was enacted. In 1942, a "Victory" tax on individual incomes was enacted. Policy makers were aware of the complications caused by these different types of taxes and, in several tax bills, attempted to rationalize these different taxes and reduce the administrative burden on taxpayers. For a summary of income tax rates and exemptions since 1913, see Joseph A. Pechman, Federal Tax Policy, Fifth Edition, Appendix A, 1987

- reduced exemption amount for each dependent from $400 to $350

Current Tax Payment Act of 1943
- imposed withholding of income tax by employers on wages paid
- canceled 75-100% of lower of 1942 or 1943 individual income tax liability

Revenue Act of 1943
- increased excise taxes on alcohol, jewelry, telephones, admissions, etc.
- increased excess profits tax rate from 90% to 95%
- lowered Victory tax rate from 5% to 3% and repealed postwar credit

Individual Income Tax Act of 1944
- raised individual income taxes
- repealed 3% Victory tax
- standardized value of personal exemptions at $500 per person

Revenue Act of 1945
- repealed excess profits tax
- reduced individual income tax rates 3 percentage points and 5% (top rate fell from 94% to 86.45%)
- reduced corporate tax rates (top rate dropped from 40% to 38%)

Revenue Act of 1948
- reduced individual income tax rates 5-13%
- increased personal exemption amount from $500 to $600
- permitted married couples to split their incomes for tax purposes
- provided additional exemption for taxpayers age 65 and over

Revenue Act of 1950
- eliminated portion of the individual income tax rate reductions from 1945 and 1948 Acts
- eliminated 53% corporate tax rate "bubble;" increased top corporate rate from 38% to 45%

Excess Profits Tax of 1950
- increased top corporate tax rate from 45% to 47%
- created temporary excess profits tax of 30% (thru 6/30/53)

Revenue Act of 1951
- temporarily increased individual income tax rates (thru 1953)
- temporarily increased corporate tax rates 5 percentage points (thru 3/31/54)
- temporarily increased excise taxes on alcohol, tobacco, gasoline, and autos (thru 3/31/54)

Excise Tax Reduction Act of 1954
- temporarily extended 1951 excise tax increases (thru 3/31/55)
- reduced excise tax rates on telephones, admissions, jewelry, etc.

Internal Revenue Code of 1954
- temporarily extended 5 percentage point increase in corporate tax rates (thru 3/31/55)
- increased depreciation deductions by providing additional depreciation schedules
- created 4% dividend tax credit for individuals

Revenue Act of 1962
- established 7% investment tax credit
- required information reporting to government for interest and dividend payments

Revenue Act of 1964
- reduced individual tax rates (top rate dropped from 91% to 70%)
- reduced top corporate tax rate from 52% to 48%
- phased-in acceleration of corporate estimated tax payments (thru 1970)

- created minimum standard deduction of $300 + $100/exemption (total $1,000 max)

Tax Adjustment Act of 1966

- **accelerated scheduled acceleration of corporate estimated tax payments**

Revenue and Expenditure Control Act of 1968

- created temporary 10% income tax surcharge on individuals (thru 6/30/69)
- created temporary 10% income tax surcharge on corporations (thru 6/30/69)
- delayed scheduled reduction in telephone and auto excise taxes

Tax Reform Act of 1969

- phased-in increase in personal exemption amount from $600 to $750
- repealed investment tax credit
- increased minimum standard deduction from $300 plus $100/capita (total max $1,000) to $1,000
- phased-in increase in percentage standard deduction from 10% to 15%
- temporarily extended income tax surcharge at 5% annual rate (thru 6/30/70)
- established individual and corporate minimum taxes
- established new tax rate schedule for single taxpayers
- delayed scheduled reduction in telephone and auto excise taxes
- lowered maximum tax rate on earned income from 70% to 50%

Revenue Act of 1971

- reinstated investment tax credit (no basis adjustment)
- repealed 7% auto excise tax, which was due to phase-out in 1982
- replaced 3/4-year depreciation convention with ½-year convention
- increased minimum standard deduction from $1,000 to $1,300
- accelerated scheduled increases in personal exemption amount and percentage standard deduction

Tax Reduction Act of 1975

- provided 10% rebate on 1974 tax liability ($200 cap)
- created temporary $30 general tax credit for each taxpayer and dependent
- temporarily increased investment tax credit to 10% (thru 1976)
- temporarily increased minimum standard deduction to $1,900 (joints) (1 year, 1975)
- temporarily increased percentage standard deduction to 16% (1 year, 1975)

Tax Reform Act of 1976

- increased percentage standard deduction to 16% ($2,800 max) and minimum s.d. to $2,100 (joints)
- temporarily extended general tax credit (max of $35/capita or 2% of $9,000 of income)(thru 1977)
- delayed decrease in investment tax credit from 10% to 7% (thru 1980)
- expanded individual minimum tax
- created unified rate schedule for estate and gift taxes with $175,000 exemption
- temporarily lowered small business tax rates (thru 1977)
- increased long-term capital gains holding period from 6 months to 1 year

Tax Reduction and Simplification Act of 1977

- replaced percentage standard deduction (s.d.) and minimum s.d. with single s.d. of $3,200 (joints)
- temporarily extended general tax credit (max of $35/capita or 2% of $9,000 of income)(thru 1978)

Revenue Act of 1978

- reduced individual taxes (widened tax brackets and reduced number of tax rates)
- increased personal exemption amount from $750 to $1,000
- reduced corporate tax rates (top rate dropped from 48% to 46%)

- increased standard deduction from $3,200 to $3,400 (joints)
- increased capital gains exclusion from 50% to 60%
- repealed nonbusiness deduction for state and local gasoline taxes

Crude Oil Windfall Profit Tax Act of 1980
- created temporary excise tax on crude oil profits (phased-out by end of 1993)
- created several business energy tax credits
- temporarily increased $200 dividend exclusion (joints) to $400 and expanded to include interest

Economic Recovery Tax Act of 1981
- phased-in 23% cut in individual tax rates; top rate dropped from 70% to 50%
- accelerated depreciation deductions; replaced depreciation system with ACRS
- indexed individual income tax parameters (beginning in 1985)
- created 10% exclusion on income for two-earner married couples ($3,000 cap)
- phased-in increase in estate tax exemption from $175,625 to $600,000 in 1987
- reduced Windfall Profit taxes
- allowed all working taxpayers to establish IRAs
- expanded provisions for employee stock ownership plans (ESOPs)
- replaced $200 interest exclusion with 15% net interest exclusion ($900 cap) (begin in 1985)

Tax Equity and Fiscal Responsibility Act of 1982
- repealed scheduled increases in accelerated depreciation deductions
- tightened safe harbor leasing rules
- required taxpayers to reduce basis by 50% of investment tax credit
- instituted 10% withholding on dividends and interest paid to individuals
- tightened completed contract accounting rules
- increased FUTA wage base and tax rate

Highway Revenue Act of 1982
- temporarily increased gasoline excise tax from 4 cents to 9 cents (thru 9/30/88)

Social Security Amendments of 1983
- accelerated scheduled increases in Social Security payroll tax rate
- instituted taxation of some Social Security benefits
- raised self-employed OASDHI rate to combined employee-employer rate, with SECA credit
- extended mandatory Social Security coverage to non-profit and new federal employees

Interest and Dividend Tax Compliance Act of 1983
- repealed scheduled 10% withholding on dividends and interest paid to individuals

Deficit Reduction Act of 1984
- repealed scheduled 15% net interest exclusion ($900 cap)
- reduced benefits from income averaging
- reduced tax benefits for property leased by tax-exempt entities
- temporarily extended telephone excise tax (thru 1987)
- increased depreciation lives for real property from 15 years to 18 years

Consolidated Omnibus Budget Reconciliation Act of 1985
- permanently increased cigarette excise tax to 16 cents per pack
- extended Medicare coverage to new state and local employees

Tax Reform Act of 1986
- reduced individual income tax rates (top rate 28%) and repealed capital gains exclusion

- repealed investment tax credit
- lowered corporation income tax rates; top rate lowered to 34 percent
- increased personal exemption amount from $1,080 to $2,000
- set uniform capitalization rules for manufacturing or construction
- increased standard deduction from $3,670 to $5,000 (joints)
- limited deduction for nonbusiness interest
- repealed second earner deduction
- limited passive losses
- established income limits on use of IRAs for taxpayers covered by pensions
- revised corporate minimum tax
- repealed sales tax deduction for individuals
- set 2-percent floor on miscellaneous itemized deductions

Omnibus Budget Reconciliation Act of 1987
- repealed installment method for dealers
- temporarily extended telephone excise tax (thru 1990)
- eliminated ESOP estate tax deduction loophole

Omnibus Budget Reconciliation Act of 1989
- modified employee stock ownership plans (ESOPs)
- established excise tax on ozone-depleting chemicals

Omnibus Budget Reconciliation Act of 1990
- increased income cap on Medicare taxes to from $53,400 to $125,000
- temporarily extended and increased gasoline tax (thru 9/30/95)
- created new 31% individual tax rate; capped capital gains rate at 28%
- permanently extended telephone excise tax
- temporarily limited itemized deductions (thru 1995)
- temporarily extended and increased air transportation excise taxes (thru 1995)
- temporarily phased-out personal exemptions (thru 1995)

Omnibus Budget Reconciliation Act of 1993
- created 36% and 39.6% tax rates for individuals
- repealed income cap on Medicare taxes
- increased transportation fuels taxes by 4.3 cents per gallon
- increased taxable portion of Social Security benefits
- permanently extended phase-out of personal exemption and limit on itemized deductions
- created 35% tax rate for corporations

Small Business Job Protection Act of 1996
- reduced possessions tax credit
- phased-in increase in small business expensing limit

Tax Relief Act of 1997
- established $500 child tax credit
- established HOPE and Lifetime Learning education tax credits
- extended air transportation excise taxes
- phased-in increase in estate tax exemption equivalent from $600,000 to $1 million in 2006
- lowered top capital gains rate from 28% to 20%
- established Roth IRAs; increased income limits for deductible IRAs

- conformed AMT depreciation lives to regular tax lives
- phased-in 15-cent per pack increase in cigarette tax
- established education IRAs

Economic Growth and Tax Relief Reconciliation Act of 2001
- phased-in lowering of individual tax rates; top tax rate became 35% (thru 2010)
- created new 10% individual tax rate (thru 2010)
- phased-in increase in child tax credit to $1,000 (thru 2010)
- phased-in increase of estate tax exemption equivalent and repeal of the estate tax (thru 2010)
- phased-in marriage penalty relief provisions (thru 2010)
- phased-in repeal of limit on itemized deductions (Pease) (thru 2010)
- phased-in increase in IRA contribution limit to $5,000 (thru 2010)
- increased individual AMT exemption to $49,000 ($35,750) for joint (single) returns (thru 2004)
- phased-in repeal of limit on personal exemptions (thru 2010)
- created above-the-line deduction for higher education expenses (thru 2005)
- increased Education IRA contribution limit to $2,000 (thru 2010)

Job Creation and Worker Assistance Act of 2002
- created 30% expensing for certain capital asset purchases (thru September 2004)
- extended of exception under Subpart F for active financing income (thru 2006)
- increased carryback of net operating losses to 5 years (thru September 2003)

Jobs and Growth Tax Relief and Reconciliation Act of 2003
- lowered top individual income tax rate on dividends to 15%/5%/0% (thru 2008)
- accelerated the 2006 tax cuts from EGTRRA
- accelerated marriage penalty relief provisions from EGTRRA (thru 2004)
- accelerated child tax credit increase to $1,000 (thru 2004)
- increased individual AMT exemption to $58,000 ($40,250) for joint (single) returns (thru 2004)
- lowered top tax rate on capital gains to 15%/5%/0% (thru 2008)
- accelerated expansion of 10% individual income tax rate bracket (thru 2004)
- increased expensing for certain capital asset purchases to 50% (thru 2004)

Working Families Tax Relief Act of 2004
- extended JGTRRA child credit tax increase (thru 2009)
- extended JGTRRA expansion of 10% individual income tax rate bracket (thru 2010)
- extended JGTRRA AMT exemption increase (thru 2005)
- extended JGTRRA marriage penalty relief provisions (thru 2008)

American Jobs Creation Act of 2004
- created deduction for income from U.S. production activities
- repealed exclusion for extraterritorial income
- changed interest expense allocation rules

Tax Increase Prevention and Reconciliation Act of 2005 (enacted in 2006)
- extended JGTRRA 15%/5%/0% dividends tax rate to 2010
- extended JGTRRA 15%/5%/0% capital gains tax rate to 2010
- increased individual AMT exemption to $62,550 ($42,500) for joint (single) returns (thru 2006)

TABLE 1 - REVENUE EFFECTS OF MAJOR BILLS ENACTED BETWEEN 1940 AND 1968

Tax bill	Treasury full-year estimates unless otherwise noted			
	Current dollars	Constant 1992 dollars	% of GDP	% of federal receipts
	($ billions)			
Revenue Act of 1940 2/	1.2	9.7	0.91	15.3
Second Revenue Act of 1940 1/ 3/	0.9	7.6	0.71	11.6
Revenue Act of 1941	3.6	27.5	2.20	32.1
Revenue Act of 1942 /2	10.0	73.4	5.04	71.4
Current Tax Payment Act of 1943 1/	2.5	18.2	1.16	6.2
Revenue Act of 1943 1/	1.0	7.3	0.46	2.4
Individual Income Tax Act of 1944 1/	-0.6	-4.2	-0.27	-1.3
Revenue Act of 1945	-5.9	-41.4	-2.67	-13.1
Revenue Act of 1948 3/	-5.0	-26.6	-1.87	-11.3
Revenue Act of 1950 2/	4.5	22.2	1.33	9.6
Excess Profits Tax of 1950 2/	3.3	16.3	0.97	6.8
Revenue Act of 1951	5.4	26.3	1.52	9.0
Excise Tax Reduction Act of 1954 2/	-1.0	-4.6	-0.24	-1.5
Internal Revenue Code of 1954 3/	-0.2	-0.8	-0.04	-0.2
Revenue Act of 1962	-0.2	-0.7	-0.03	-0.2
Revenue Act of 1964	-11.5	-44.6	-1.60	-9.0
Tax Adjustment Act of 1966 2/ 3/	5.0	18.2	0.60	3.5

1/ Joint Committee on Taxation (JCT) estimate; before 1974, JCT was called Joint Committee on Internal Revenue Taxation
2/ Estimate is from Congressional Record; unclear if estimate is from Treasury or JCT
3/ Estimate is for year after enactment

TABLE 2 - REVENUE EFFECTS OF MAJOR BILLS ENACTED SINCE 1968

	Tax bill	Number of years after enactment				First-2-yr average	4-year average
		1	2	3	4		
		Current dollars (in billions)					
1	Revenue and Expenditure Control Act of 1968	16.0	4.7	N/A	N/A	10.4	N/A
2	Tax Reform Act of 1969	3.8	2.4	N/A	N/A	3.1	N/A
3	Revenue Act of 1971	-4.4	-6 9	N/A	N/A	-5.7	N/A
4	Tax Reduction Act of 1975	-9.8	0.4	N/A	N/A	-4.7	N/A
5	Tax Reform Act of 1976	-15.3	-11 9	-7.1	N/A	-13.6	N/A
6	Tax Reduction and Simplification Act of 1977	-17.8	-13.7	-5.8	N/A	-15.8	N/A
7	Revenue Act of 1978	-11.5	-22 8	-26.7	-30 6	-17.2	-22.9
8	Crude Oil Windfall Profit Tax Act of 1980	13.0	18.4	18.8	21 0	15.7	17.8
9	Economic Recovery Tax Act of 1981	-38.3	-91 6	-139.0	-176.7	-65.0	-111.4
10	Tax Equity and Fiscal Responsibility Act of 1982	17.3	38.3	42.2	52.1	27.8	37.5
11	Highway Revenue Act of 1982	1.7	3.8	3.9	3 9	2.8	3.3
12	Social Security Amendments of 1983	6.2	8 8	9.3	11.4	7.5	8.9
13	Interest and Dividend Tax Compliance Act of 1983	-2.6	-2.4	-2.1	-1.7	-2.5	-2.2
14	Deficit Reduction Act of 1984	9.3	15 9	21.6	24 6	12.6	17.9
15	Consolidated Omnibus Budget Reconciliation Act of 1985	0.9	2.7	3.0	3 0	1.8	2.4
16	Tax Reform Act of 1986	18.6	0.9	-11.7	-9 0	9.8	-0.3
17	Omnibus Budget Reconciliation Act of 1987	9.1	14 3	16.2	15 6	11.7	13.8
18	Omnibus Budget Reconciliation Act of 1989	5.7	3.5	3.6	5.4	4.6	4.6
19	Omnibus Budget Reconciliation Act of 1990	23.2	35.0	31.9	36 5	29.1	31.7
20	Omnibus Budget Reconciliation Act of 1993	24.3	45.3	52.5	65 9	34.8	47.0
21	Small Business Job Protection Act of 1996	-0.6	-0 6	0.1	0 2	-0.6	-0.3
22	Tax Relief Act of 1997	-9.4	-3.8	-18.6	-20 9	-6.6	-13.2
23	Economic Growth and Tax Relief Reconciliation Act of 2001	-34.4	-85.5	-104.0	-103.7	-60.0	-81.9
24	Job Creation and Worker Assistance Act of 2002	-46.0	-27 3	3.8	20 8	-36.7	-12.2
25	Jobs and Growth Tax Relief Reconciliation Act of 2003	-136.6	-78.0	-8.9	-1.4	-107.3	-56.2
26	Working Familes Tax Relief Act of 2004	-27.2	-40 3	-20.4	-15.7	-33.8	-25.9
27	American Jobs Creation Act of 2004	-3.3	-4 5	-5.9	-23 5	-3.9	-9.3
28	Tax Increase Prevention and Reconciliation Act of 2005 (enacted in 2006)	-35.4	-4.8	-39.6	-7 9	-20.1	-21.9
		Constant 1992 dollars (in billions)					
1	Revenue and Expenditure Control Act of 1968	55.3	15.4	N/A	N/A	35.4	N/A
2	Tax Reform Act of 1969	12.5	7 5	N/A	N/A	10.0	N/A
3	Revenue Act of 1971	-13.2	-19 5	N/A	N/A	-16.4	N/A
4	Tax Reduction Act of 1975	-21.9	0 8	N/A	N/A	-10.5	N/A
5	Tax Reform Act of 1976	-32.4	-23 8	-13.5	N/A	-28.1	N/A
6	Tax Reduction and Simplification Act of 1977	-35.5	-25 8	-10.3	N/A	-30.6	N/A
7	Revenue Act of 1978	-21.0	-39 0	-43.2	-47.4	-30.0	-37.6
8	Crude Oil Windfall Profit Tax Act of 1980	19.8	25.7	24.2	25.1	22.8	23.7
9	Economic Recovery Tax Act of 1981	-54.9	-123.7	-178.9	-217 2	-89.3	-143.7
10	Tax Equity and Fiscal Responsibility Act of 1982	23.7	50.0	52.5	61 9	36.8	47.0
11	Highway Revenue Act of 1982	2.3	5.0	4.9	4 6	3.6	4.2
12	Social Security Amendments of 1983	8.2	11.1	11.3	13 3	9.7	11.0
13	Interest and Dividend Tax Compliance Act of 1983	-3.5	-3.0	-2.5	-2 0	-3.2	-2.8
14	Deficit Reduction Act of 1984	12.0	19.7	25.6	28.1	15.8	21.3
15	Consolidated Omnibus Budget Reconciliation Act of 1985	1.1	3.2	3.5	3.4	2.2	2.8
16	Tax Reform Act of 1986	22.4	1.0	-13.1	-9 8	11.7	0.1
17	Omnibus Budget Reconciliation Act of 1987	10.7	16.2	17.7	16.5	13.4	15.3
18	Omnibus Budget Reconciliation Act of 1989	6.2	3.6	3.6	5.2	4.9	4.7
19	Omnibus Budget Reconciliation Act of 1990	24.1	34.9	30.7	33.9	29.5	30.9
20	Omnibus Budget Reconciliation Act of 1993	22.9	41.6	46.9	57.1	32.3	42.1
21	Small Business Job Protection Act of 1996	-0.6	-0 5	0.1	0.1	-0.6	-0.2
22	Tax Relief Act of 1997	-8.2	-3 3	-15.6	-17.1	-5.7	-11.0
23	Economic Growth and Tax Relief Reconciliation Act of 2001	-28.3	-69.1	-82.6	-80 8	-48.7	-65.2
24	Job Creation and Worker Assistance Act of 2002	-37.7	-22 0	3.0	16 2	-29.9	-10.1
25	Jobs and Growth Tax Relief Reconciliation Act of 2003	-110.2	-62.1	-7.0	-1.1	-86.1	-45.1
26	Working Familes Tax Relief Act of 2004	-21.5	-31.4	-15.6	-11 8	-26.4	-20.1
27	American Jobs Creation Act of 2004	-2.6	-3 5	-4.5	-17 6	-3.0	-7.1
28	Tax Increase Prevention and Reconciliation Act of 2005 (enacted in 2006)	-26.4	-3 5	-28.2	-5 5	-15.0	-15.9

TABLE 2 - REVENUE EFFECTS OF MAJOR BILLS ENACTED SINCE 1968
(CONTINUED)

	Tax bill	Number of years after enactment				First-2-yr average	4-year average
		1	2	3	4		
		Revenue effect as percentage of GDP					
1	Revenue and Expenditure Control Act of 1968	1.74	0.45	N/A	N/A	1 09	N/A
2	Tax Reform Act of 1969	0.39	0.21	N/A	N/A	0 30	N/A
3	Revenue Act of 1971	-0.38	-0.50	N/A	N/A	-0.44	N/A
4	Tax Reduction Act of 1975	-0.58	0.02	N/A	N/A	-0 28	N/A
5	Tax Reform Act of 1976	-0.81	-0.57	-0 30	N/A	-0 69	N/A
6	Tax Reduction and Simplification Act of 1977	-0.85	-0.59	-0 22	N/A	-0.72	N/A
7	Revenue Act of 1978	-0.49	-0.89	-0 95	-0.99	-0 69	-0 83
8	Crude Oil Windfall Profit Tax Act of 1980	0.44	0.56	0 51	0.51	0 50	0 50
9	Economic Recovery Tax Act of 1981	-1.21	-2.60	-3 58	-4.15	-1 91	-2 89
10	Tax Equity and Fiscal Responsibility Act of 1982	0.53	1.07	1 08	1.23	0 80	0 98
11	Highway Revenue Act of 1982	0.05	0.11	0.10	0.09	0 08	0 09
12	Social Security Amendments of 1983	0.17	0.22	0 22	0.24	0 20	0 21
13	Interest and Dividend Tax Compliance Act of 1983	-0.07	-0.06	-0 05	-0.04	-0 07	-0 05
14	Deficit Reduction Act of 1984	0.24	0.37	0.47	0.49	0 30	0 39
15	Consolidated Omnibus Budget Reconciliation Act of 1985	0.02	0.06	0 06	0.06	0 04	0 05
16	Tax Reform Act of 1986	0.41	0.02	-0 23	-0.16	0 22	0 01
17	Omnibus Budget Reconciliation Act of 1987	0.19	0.28	0 30	0.27	0 24	0 26
18	Omnibus Budget Reconciliation Act of 1989	0.10	0.06	0 06	0.08	0 08	0 07
19	Omnibus Budget Reconciliation Act of 1990	0.41	0.57	0.49	0.52	0.49	0 50
20	Omnibus Budget Reconciliation Act of 1993	0.36	0.64	0.70	0.83	0 50	0 63
21	Small Business Job Protection Act of 1996	-0.01	-0.01	0 00	0.00	-0 01	0 00
22	Tax Relief Act of 1997	-0.11	-0.04	-0 20	-0.22	-0 08	-0.14
23	Economic Growth and Tax Relief Reconciliation Act of 2001	-0.33	-0.77	-0 89	-0.84	-0 55	-0.71
24	Job Creation and Worker Assistance Act of 2002	-0.42	-0.24	0 03	0.16	-0 33	-0.12
25	Jobs and Growth Tax Relief Reconciliation Act of 2003	-1.19	-0.65	-0 07	-0.01	-0 92	-0.48
26	Working Familes Tax Relief Act of 2004	-0.22	-0.32	-0.15	-0.11	-0 27	-0.20
27	American Jobs Creation Act of 2004	-0.03	-0.04	-0 04	-0.17	-0 03	-0 07
28	Tax Increase Prevention and Reconciliation Act of 2005 (enacted in 2006)	-0.27	-0.03	-0 27	-0.05	-0.15	-0.15
		Percentage change in federal receipts because of tax bill					
1	Revenue and Expenditure Control Act of 1968	9.4	2 6	N/A	N/A	6.0	N/A
2	Tax Reform Act of 1969	1.9	1 2	N/A	N/A	1.6	N/A
3	Revenue Act of 1971	-2.2	-3 0	N/A	N/A	-2.6	N/A
4	Tax Reduction Act of 1975	-3.2	0.1	N/A	N/A	-1.5	N/A
5	Tax Reform Act of 1976	-4.1	-2 8	-1.5	N/A	-3.5	N/A
6	Tax Reduction and Simplification Act of 1977	-4.3	-3 2	-1.2	N/A	-3.7	N/A
7	Revenue Act of 1978	-2.5	-4 3	-4.5	-4 5	-3.4	-3.9
8	Crude Oil Windfall Profit Tax Act of 1980	2.2	2.7	2.4	2 3	2.4	2.4
9	Economic Recovery Tax Act of 1981	-5.7	-12 3	-16.5	-18 6	-9.0	-13.3
10	Tax Equity and Fiscal Responsibility Act of 1982	3.0	6 3	6.3	7 2	4.6	5.7
11	Highway Revenue Act of 1982	0.3	0 6	0.5	0 5	0.4	0.5
12	Social Security Amendments of 1983	0.9	1 2	1.2	1 3	1.1	1.2
13	Interest and Dividend Tax Compliance Act of 1983	-0.4	-0 3	-0.3	-0 2	-0.4	-0.3
14	Deficit Reduction Act of 1984	1.3	2 0	2.6	2.7	1.7	2.1
15	Consolidated Omnibus Budget Reconciliation Act of 1985	0.1	0 3	0.3	0 3	0.2	0.3
16	Tax Reform Act of 1986	2.3	0.1	-1.2	-0 9	1.2	0.1
17	Omnibus Budget Reconciliation Act of 1987	1.0	1 5	1.6	1.4	1.3	1.4
18	Omnibus Budget Reconciliation Act of 1989	0.5	0 3	0.3	0.4	0.4	0.4
19	Omnibus Budget Reconciliation Act of 1990	2.2	3.1	2.6	2.7	2.6	2.7
20	Omnibus Budget Reconciliation Act of 1993	2.0	3 5	3.9	4.7	2.7	3.5
21	Small Business Job Protection Act of 1996	0.0	0 0	0.0	0 0	0.0	0.0
22	Tax Relief Act of 1997	-0.6	-0 2	-1.0	-1.1	-0.4	-0.7
23	Economic Growth and Tax Relief Reconciliation Act of 2001	-1.7	-3 9	-4.4	-4 2	-2.8	-3.6
24	Job Creation and Worker Assistance Act of 2002	-2.4	-1 3	0.2	0 9	-1.9	-0.7
25	Jobs and Growth Tax Relief Reconciliation Act of 2003	-6.3	-3.4	-0.4	-0.1	-4.8	-2.5
26	Working Familes Tax Relief Act of 2004	-1.3	-1 8	-0.9	-0 6	-1.6	-1.1
27	American Jobs Creation Act of 2004	-0.2	-0 2	-0.3	-0 9	-0.2	-0.4
28	Tax Increase Prevention and Reconciliation Act of 2005 (enacted in 2006)	-1.5	-0 2	-1.5	-0 3	-0.8	-0.8

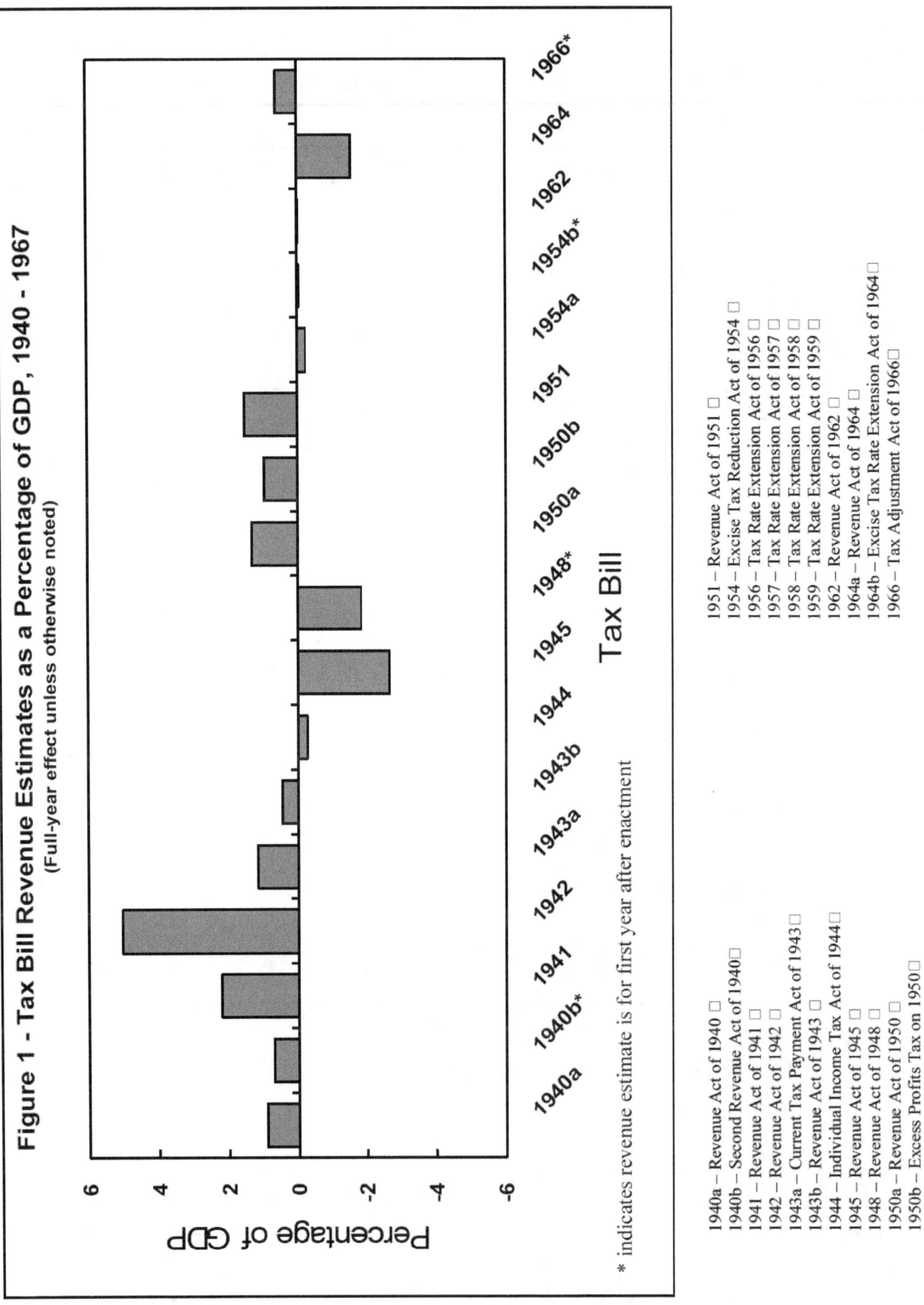

Figure 1 - Tax Bill Revenue Estimates as a Percentage of GDP, 1940 - 1967
(Full-year effect unless otherwise noted)

* indicates revenue estimate is for first year after enactment

1940a – Revenue Act of 1940
1940b – Second Revenue Act of 1940
1941 – Revenue Act of 1941
1942 – Revenue Act of 1942
1943a – Current Tax Payment Act of 1943
1943b – Revenue Act of 1943
1944 – Individual Income Tax Act of 1944
1945 – Revenue Act of 1945
1948 – Revenue Act of 1948
1950a – Revenue Act of 1950
1950b – Excess Profits Tax on 1950

1951 – Revenue Act of 1951
1954 – Excise Tax Reduction Act of 1954
1956 – Tax Rate Extension Act of 1956
1957 – Tax Rate Extension Act of 1957
1958 – Tax Rate Extension Act of 1958
1959 – Tax Rate Extension Act of 1959
1962 – Revenue Act of 1962
1964a – Revenue Act of 1964
1964b – Excise Tax Rate Extension Act of 1964
1966 – Tax Adjustment Act of 1966

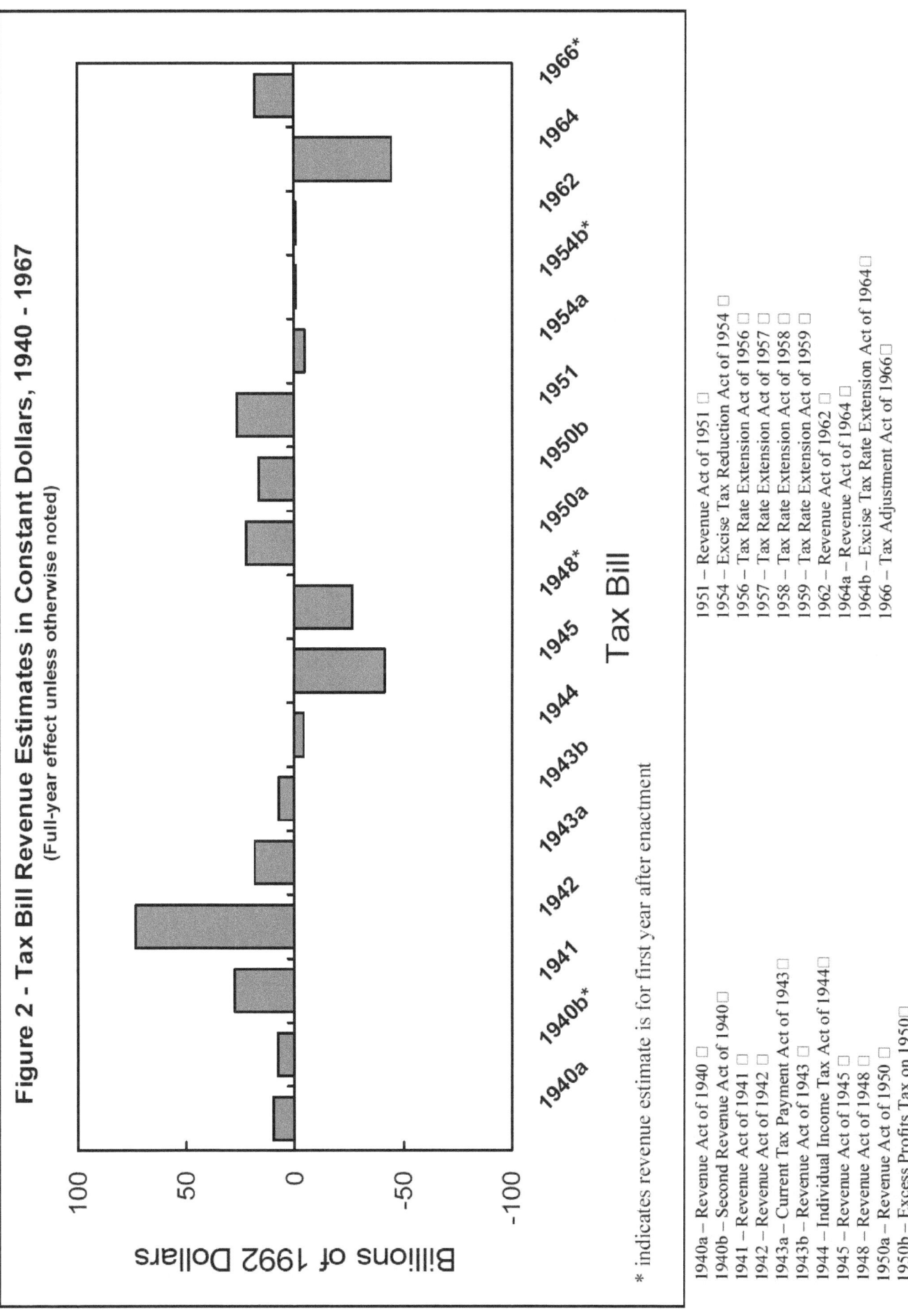

Figure 2 - Tax Bill Revenue Estimates in Constant Dollars, 1940 - 1967
(Full-year effect unless otherwise noted)

* indicates revenue estimate is for first year after enactment

1940a – Revenue Act of 1940
1940b – Second Revenue Act of 1940
1941 – Revenue Act of 1941
1942 – Revenue Act of 1942
1943a – Current Tax Payment Act of 1943
1943b – Revenue Act of 1943
1944 – Individual Income Tax Act of 1944
1945 – Revenue Act of 1945
1948 – Revenue Act of 1948
1950a – Revenue Act of 1950
1950b – Excess Profits Tax on 1950

1951 – Revenue Act of 1951
1954 – Excise Tax Reduction Act of 1954
1956 – Tax Rate Extension Act of 1956
1957 – Tax Rate Extension Act of 1957
1958 – Tax Rate Extension Act of 1958
1959 – Tax Rate Extension Act of 1959
1962 – Revenue Act of 1962
1964a – Revenue Act of 1964
1964b – Excise Tax Rate Extension Act of 1964
1966 – Tax Adjustment Act of 1966

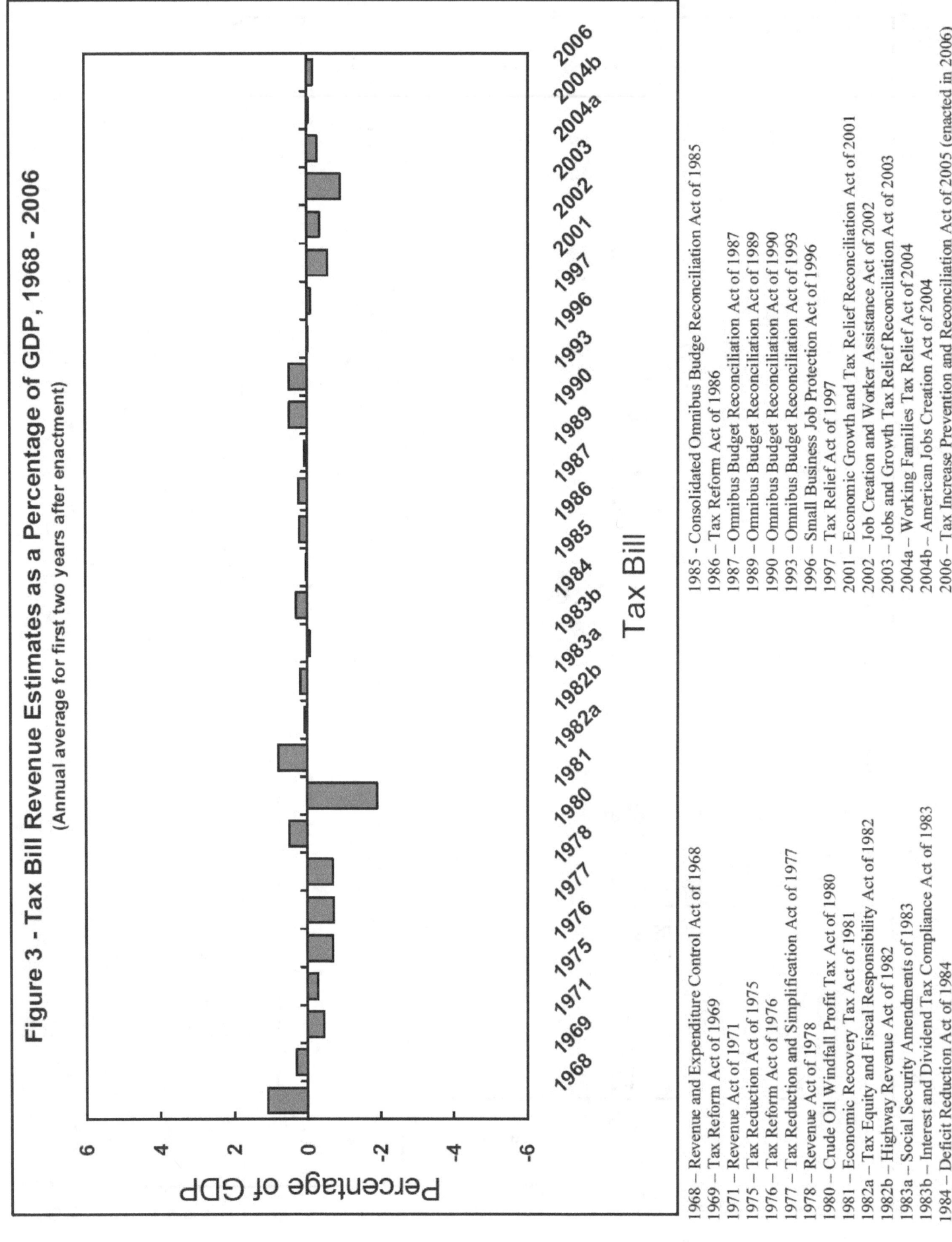

Figure 3 - Tax Bill Revenue Estimates as a Percentage of GDP, 1968 - 2006
(Annual average for first two years after enactment)

1968 – Revenue and Expenditure Control Act of 1968
1969 – Tax Reform Act of 1969
1971 – Revenue Act of 1971
1975 – Tax Reduction Act of 1975
1976 – Tax Reform Act of 1976
1977 – Tax Reduction and Simplification Act of 1977
1978 – Revenue Act of 1978
1980 – Crude Oil Windfall Profit Tax Act of 1980
1981 – Economic Recovery Tax Act of 1981
1982a – Tax Equity and Fiscal Responsibility Act of 1982
1982b – Highway Revenue Act of 1982
1983a – Social Security Amendments of 1983
1983b – Interest and Dividend Tax Compliance Act of 1983
1984 – Deficit Reduction Act of 1984

1985 - Consolidated Omnibus Budge Reconciliation Act of 1985
1986 – Tax Reform Act of 1986
1987 – Omnibus Budget Reconciliation Act of 1987
1989 – Omnibus Budget Reconciliation Act of 1989
1990 – Omnibus Budget Reconciliation Act of 1990
1993 – Omnibus Budget Reconciliation Act of 1993
1996 – Small Business Job Protection Act of 1996
1997 – Tax Relief Act of 1997
2001 – Economic Growth and Tax Relief Reconciliation Act of 2001
2002 – Job Creation and Worker Assistance Act of 2002
2003 – Jobs and Growth Tax Relief Reconciliation Act of 2003
2004a – Working Families Tax Relief Act of 2004
2004b – American Jobs Creation Act of 2004
2006 – Tax Increase Prevention and Reconciliation Act of 2005 (enacted in 2006)

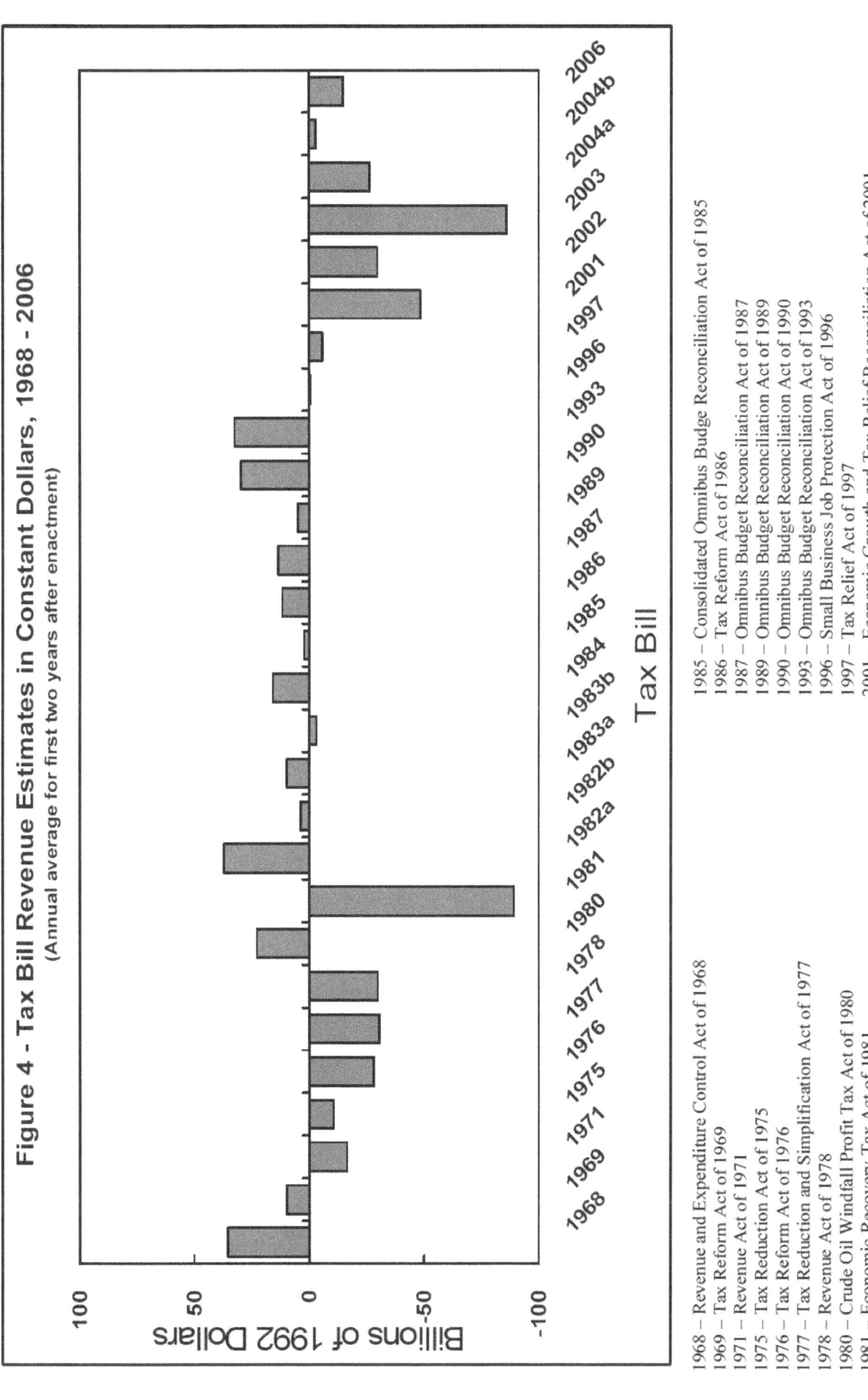

Figure 4 - Tax Bill Revenue Estimates in Constant Dollars, 1968 - 2006
(Annual average for first two years after enactment)

1968 – Revenue and Expenditure Control Act of 1968
1969 – Tax Reform Act of 1969
1971 – Revenue Act of 1971
1975 – Tax Reduction Act of 1975
1976 – Tax Reform Act of 1976
1977 – Tax Reduction and Simplification Act of 1977
1978 – Revenue Act of 1978
1980 – Crude Oil Windfall Profit Tax Act of 1980
1981 – Economic Recovery Tax Act of 1981
1982a – Tax Equity and Fiscal Responsibility Act of 1982
1982b – Highway Revenue Act of 1982
1983a – Social Security Amendments of 1983
1983b – Interest and Dividend Tax Compliance Act of 1983
1984 – Deficit Reduction Act of 1984

1985 – Consolidated Omnibus Budge Reconciliation Act of 1985
1986 – Tax Reform Act of 1986
1987 – Omnibus Budget Reconciliation Act of 1987
1989 – Omnibus Budget Reconciliation Act of 1989
1990 – Omnibus Budget Reconciliation Act of 1990
1993 – Omnibus Budget Reconciliation Act of 1993
1996 – Small Business Job Protection Act of 1996
1997 – Tax Relief Act of 1997
2001 – Economic Growth and Tax Relief Reconciliation Act of 2001
2002 – Job Creation and Worker Assistance Act of 2002
2003 – Jobs and Growth Tax Relief Reconciliation Act of 2003
2004a – Working Families Tax Relief Act of 2004
2004b – American Jobs Creation Act of 2004
2006 – Tax Increase Prevention and Reconciliation Act of 2005 (enacted in 2006)